THIS JOURNAL BELONGS TO

____

____

BY OLIVIA BROOKS

Start Date: _______________   **End Date:** _______________

THE BOOK I READ IS...

THE AUTHOR IS...

THE STORY IS ABOUT...

MY FAVORITE CHARACTER IS ...

BECAUSE ...

WHAT I LIKED ABOUT THIS
STORY IS...

WHAT I DISLIKED ABOUT THIS
STORY IS...

I THINK THIS BOOK IS...

WHICH IS WHY I GIVE IT THIS MANY STARS

WOULD I READ IT AGAIN?

Start Date: _______________   End Date: _______________

THE BOOK I READ IS...

THE AUTHOR IS...

THE STORY IS ABOUT...

MY FAVORITE CHARACTER IS ...

BECAUSE ...

WHAT I LIKED ABOUT THIS
STORY IS...

WHAT I DISLIKED ABOUT THIS
STORY IS...

I THINK THIS BOOK IS...

WHICH IS WHY I GIVE IT THIS MANY STARS

WOULD I READ IT AGAIN?

Start Date: ___________________   **End Date:** ___________________

THE BOOK I READ IS...

THE AUTHOR IS...

THE STORY IS ABOUT...

MY FAVORITE CHARACTER IS ...

BECAUSE ...

WHAT I LIKED ABOUT THIS
STORY IS...

WHAT I DISLIKED ABOUT THIS
STORY IS...

I THINK THIS BOOK IS...

WHICH IS WHY I GIVE IT THIS MANY STARS

WOULD I READ IT AGAIN?

Start Date: ______________   End Date: _______________

THE BOOK I READ IS...

THE AUTHOR IS...

THE STORY IS ABOUT...

MY FAVORITE CHARACTER IS ...

BECAUSE ...

WHAT I LIKED ABOUT THIS
STORY IS...

WHAT I DISLIKED ABOUT THIS
STORY IS...

I THINK THIS BOOK IS...

WHICH IS WHY I GIVE IT THIS MANY STARS

WOULD I READ IT AGAIN?

Start Date: _______________   End Date: _______________

THE BOOK I READ IS...

THE AUTHOR IS...

THE STORY IS ABOUT...

MY FAVORITE CHARACTER IS ...

BECAUSE ...

WHAT I LIKED ABOUT THIS
STORY IS...

WHAT I DISLIKED ABOUT THIS
STORY IS...

I THINK THIS BOOK IS...

WHICH IS WHY I GIVE IT THIS MANY STARS

WOULD I READ IT AGAIN?

Start Date: ______________   End Date: ______________

THE BOOK I READ IS...

THE AUTHOR IS...

THE STORY IS ABOUT...

MY FAVORITE CHARACTER IS ...

BECAUSE ...

WHAT I LIKED ABOUT THIS
STORY IS...

WHAT I DISLIKED ABOUT THIS
STORY IS...

I THINK THIS BOOK IS...

WHICH IS WHY I GIVE IT THIS MANY STARS

WOULD I READ IT AGAIN?

Start Date: ______________   End Date: ______________

THE BOOK I READ IS...

THE AUTHOR IS...

THE STORY IS ABOUT...

MY FAVORITE CHARACTER IS ...

BECAUSE ...

WHAT I LIKED ABOUT THIS STORY IS...

WHAT I DISLIKED ABOUT THIS STORY IS...

I THINK THIS BOOK IS...

WHICH IS WHY I GIVE IT THIS MANY STARS

WOULD I READ IT AGAIN?

Start Date: _______________   End Date: _______________

THE BOOK I READ IS...

THE AUTHOR IS...

THE STORY IS ABOUT...

MY FAVORITE CHARACTER IS ...

BECAUSE ...

WHAT I LIKED ABOUT THIS
STORY IS...

WHAT I DISLIKED ABOUT THIS
STORY IS...

I THINK THIS BOOK IS...

WHICH IS WHY I GIVE IT THIS MANY STARS

WOULD I READ IT AGAIN?

Start Date: _______________   End Date: _______________

THE BOOK I READ IS...

THE AUTHOR IS...

THE STORY IS ABOUT...

MY FAVORITE CHARACTER IS ...

BECAUSE ...

WHAT I LIKED ABOUT THIS STORY IS...

WHAT I DISLIKED ABOUT THIS STORY IS...

I THINK THIS BOOK IS...

WHICH IS WHY I GIVE IT THIS MANY STARS

WOULD I READ IT AGAIN?

Start Date: ________________   End Date: ________________

THE BOOK I READ IS...

THE AUTHOR IS...

THE STORY IS ABOUT...

MY FAVORITE CHARACTER IS ...

BECAUSE ...

WHAT I LIKED ABOUT THIS
STORY IS...

WHAT I DISLIKED ABOUT THIS
STORY IS...

I THINK THIS BOOK IS...

WHICH IS WHY I GIVE IT THIS MANY STARS

WOULD I READ IT AGAIN?

Start Date: ________________   End Date: ________________

THE BOOK I READ IS...

THE AUTHOR IS...

THE STORY IS ABOUT...

MY FAVORITE CHARACTER IS ...

BECAUSE ...

WHAT I LIKED ABOUT THIS
STORY IS...

WHAT I DISLIKED ABOUT THIS
STORY IS...

I THINK THIS BOOK IS...

WHICH IS WHY I GIVE IT THIS MANY STARS

WOULD I READ IT AGAIN?

Start Date: _______________   End Date: _______________

THE BOOK I READ IS...

THE AUTHOR IS...

THE STORY IS ABOUT...

MY FAVORITE CHARACTER IS ...

BECAUSE ...

WHAT I LIKED ABOUT THIS
STORY IS...

WHAT I DISLIKED ABOUT THIS
STORY IS...

I THINK THIS BOOK IS...

WHICH IS WHY I GIVE IT THIS MANY STARS

WOULD I READ IT AGAIN?

Start Date: _______________   **End Date:** _______________

THE BOOK I READ IS...

THE AUTHOR IS...

THE STORY IS ABOUT...

MY FAVORITE CHARACTER IS ...

BECAUSE ...

WHAT I LIKED ABOUT THIS
STORY IS...

WHAT I DISLIKED ABOUT THIS
STORY IS...

I THINK THIS BOOK IS...

WHICH IS WHY I GIVE IT THIS MANY STARS

WOULD I READ IT AGAIN?

Start Date: _______________   End Date: _______________

THE BOOK I READ IS...

THE AUTHOR IS...

THE STORY IS ABOUT...

MY FAVORITE CHARACTER IS ...

BECAUSE ...

WHAT I LIKED ABOUT THIS
STORY IS...

WHAT I DISLIKED ABOUT THIS
STORY IS...

I THINK THIS BOOK IS...

WHICH IS WHY I GIVE IT THIS MANY STARS

WOULD I READ IT AGAIN?

Start Date: ________________   End Date: ________________

THE BOOK I READ IS...

THE AUTHOR IS...

THE STORY IS ABOUT...

MY FAVORITE CHARACTER IS ...

BECAUSE ...

WHAT I LIKED ABOUT THIS
STORY IS...

WHAT I DISLIKED ABOUT THIS
STORY IS...

I THINK THIS BOOK IS...

WHICH IS WHY I GIVE IT THIS MANY STARS

WOULD I READ IT AGAIN?

Start Date: _________________   End Date: _________________

THE BOOK I READ IS...

THE AUTHOR IS...

THE STORY IS ABOUT...

MY FAVORITE CHARACTER IS ...

BECAUSE ...

WHAT I LIKED ABOUT THIS
STORY IS...

WHAT I DISLIKED ABOUT THIS
STORY IS...

I THINK THIS BOOK IS...

WHICH IS WHY I GIVE IT THIS MANY STARS

WOULD I READ IT AGAIN?

Start Date: ________________   End Date: ________________

THE BOOK I READ IS...

THE AUTHOR IS...

THE STORY IS ABOUT...

MY FAVORITE CHARACTER IS ...

BECAUSE ...

WHAT I LIKED ABOUT THIS
STORY IS...

WHAT I DISLIKED ABOUT THIS
STORY IS...

I THINK THIS BOOK IS...

WHICH IS WHY I GIVE IT THIS MANY STARS

WOULD I READ IT AGAIN?

Start Date: _______________   End Date: _______________

THE BOOK I READ IS...

THE AUTHOR IS...

THE STORY IS ABOUT...

MY FAVORITE CHARACTER IS ...

BECAUSE ...

WHAT I LIKED ABOUT THIS
STORY IS...

WHAT I DISLIKED ABOUT THIS
STORY IS...

I THINK THIS BOOK IS...

WHICH IS WHY I GIVE IT THIS MANY STARS

WOULD I READ IT AGAIN?

Start Date: _______________   End Date: _______________

THE BOOK I READ IS...

THE AUTHOR IS...

THE STORY IS ABOUT...

MY FAVORITE CHARACTER IS ...

BECAUSE ...

WHAT I LIKED ABOUT THIS STORY IS...

WHAT I DISLIKED ABOUT THIS STORY IS...

I THINK THIS BOOK IS...

WHICH IS WHY I GIVE IT THIS MANY STARS

WOULD I READ IT AGAIN?

Start Date: ______________   End Date: ______________

THE BOOK I READ IS...

THE AUTHOR IS...

THE STORY IS ABOUT...

MY FAVORITE CHARACTER IS ...

BECAUSE ...

WHAT I LIKED ABOUT THIS
STORY IS...

WHAT I DISLIKED ABOUT THIS
STORY IS...

I THINK THIS BOOK IS...

WHICH IS WHY I GIVE IT THIS MANY STARS

WOULD I READ IT AGAIN?

Start Date: _______________   End Date: _______________

THE BOOK I READ IS...

THE AUTHOR IS...

THE STORY IS ABOUT...

MY FAVORITE CHARACTER IS ...

BECAUSE ...

WHAT I LIKED ABOUT THIS
STORY IS...

WHAT I DISLIKED ABOUT THIS
STORY IS...

I THINK THIS BOOK IS...

WHICH IS WHY I GIVE IT THIS MANY STARS

WOULD I READ IT AGAIN?

Start Date: _______________   **End Date:** _______________

THE BOOK I READ IS...

THE AUTHOR IS...

THE STORY IS ABOUT...

MY FAVORITE CHARACTER IS ...

BECAUSE ...

WHAT I LIKED ABOUT THIS
STORY IS...

WHAT I DISLIKED ABOUT THIS
STORY IS...

I THINK THIS BOOK IS...

WHICH IS WHY I GIVE IT THIS MANY STARS

WOULD I READ IT AGAIN?

Start Date: ________________   End Date: ________________

THE BOOK I READ IS...

THE AUTHOR IS...

THE STORY IS ABOUT...

MY FAVORITE CHARACTER IS ...

BECAUSE ...

WHAT I LIKED ABOUT THIS
STORY IS...

WHAT I DISLIKED ABOUT THIS
STORY IS...

I THINK THIS BOOK IS...

WHICH IS WHY I GIVE IT THIS MANY STARS

WOULD I READ IT AGAIN?

Start Date: ______________   End Date: ______________

THE BOOK I READ IS...

THE AUTHOR IS...

THE STORY IS ABOUT...

MY FAVORITE CHARACTER IS ...

BECAUSE ...

WHAT I LIKED ABOUT THIS
STORY IS...

WHAT I DISLIKED ABOUT THIS
STORY IS...

I THINK THIS BOOK IS...

WHICH IS WHY I GIVE IT THIS MANY STARS

WOULD I READ IT AGAIN?

Start Date: _______________   End Date: _______________

THE BOOK I READ IS...

THE AUTHOR IS...

THE STORY IS ABOUT...

MY FAVORITE CHARACTER IS ...

BECAUSE ...

WHAT I LIKED ABOUT THIS STORY IS...

WHAT I DISLIKED ABOUT THIS STORY IS...

I THINK THIS BOOK IS...

WHICH IS WHY I GIVE IT THIS MANY STARS

WOULD I READ IT AGAIN?

Start Date: ________________   End Date: ________________

THE BOOK I READ IS...

THE AUTHOR IS...

THE STORY IS ABOUT...

MY FAVORITE CHARACTER IS ...

BECAUSE ...

WHAT I LIKED ABOUT THIS
STORY IS...

WHAT I DISLIKED ABOUT THIS
STORY IS...

I THINK THIS BOOK IS...

WHICH IS WHY I GIVE IT THIS MANY STARS

WOULD I READ IT AGAIN?

Start Date: ________________   End Date: ________________

THE BOOK I READ IS...

THE AUTHOR IS...

THE STORY IS ABOUT...

MY FAVORITE CHARACTER IS ...

BECAUSE ...

WHAT I LIKED ABOUT THIS
STORY IS...

WHAT I DISLIKED ABOUT THIS
STORY IS...

I THINK THIS BOOK IS...

WHICH IS WHY I GIVE IT THIS MANY STARS

WOULD I READ IT AGAIN?

Start Date: _______________   End Date: _______________

THE BOOK I READ IS...

THE AUTHOR IS...

THE STORY IS ABOUT...

MY FAVORITE CHARACTER IS ...

BECAUSE ...

WHAT I LIKED ABOUT THIS
STORY IS...

WHAT I DISLIKED ABOUT THIS
STORY IS...

I THINK THIS BOOK IS...

WHICH IS WHY I GIVE IT THIS MANY STARS

WOULD I READ IT AGAIN?

Start Date: ______________   End Date: ______________

THE BOOK I READ IS...

THE AUTHOR IS...

THE STORY IS ABOUT...

MY FAVORITE CHARACTER IS ...

BECAUSE ...

WHAT I LIKED ABOUT THIS
STORY IS...

WHAT I DISLIKED ABOUT THIS
STORY IS...

I THINK THIS BOOK IS...

WHICH IS WHY I GIVE IT THIS MANY STARS

WOULD I READ IT AGAIN?

Start Date: _______________   End Date: _______________

THE BOOK I READ IS...

THE AUTHOR IS...

THE STORY IS ABOUT...

MY FAVORITE CHARACTER IS ...

BECAUSE ...

WHAT I LIKED ABOUT THIS
STORY IS...

WHAT I DISLIKED ABOUT THIS
STORY IS...

I THINK THIS BOOK IS...

WHICH IS WHY I GIVE IT THIS MANY STARS

WOULD I READ IT AGAIN?

Start Date: ______________   End Date: ______________

THE BOOK I READ IS...

THE AUTHOR IS...

THE STORY IS ABOUT...

MY FAVORITE CHARACTER IS ...

BECAUSE ...

WHAT I LIKED ABOUT THIS
STORY IS...

WHAT I DISLIKED ABOUT THIS
STORY IS...

I THINK THIS BOOK IS...

WHICH IS WHY I GIVE IT THIS MANY STARS

WOULD I READ IT AGAIN?

Start Date: _________________   End Date: _________________

THE BOOK I READ IS...

THE AUTHOR IS...

THE STORY IS ABOUT...

MY FAVORITE CHARACTER IS ...

BECAUSE ...

WHAT I LIKED ABOUT THIS
STORY IS...

WHAT I DISLIKED ABOUT THIS
STORY IS...

I THINK THIS BOOK IS...

WHICH IS WHY I GIVE IT THIS MANY STARS

WOULD I READ IT AGAIN?

Start Date: _______________   End Date: _______________

THE BOOK I READ IS...

THE AUTHOR IS...

THE STORY IS ABOUT...

MY FAVORITE CHARACTER IS ...

BECAUSE ...

WHAT I LIKED ABOUT THIS
STORY IS...

WHAT I DISLIKED ABOUT THIS
STORY IS...

I THINK THIS BOOK IS...

WHICH IS WHY I GIVE IT THIS MANY STARS

WOULD I READ IT AGAIN?

Start Date: ________________   End Date: ________________

THE BOOK I READ IS...

THE AUTHOR IS...

THE STORY IS ABOUT...

MY FAVORITE CHARACTER IS ...

BECAUSE ...

WHAT I LIKED ABOUT THIS STORY IS...

WHAT I DISLIKED ABOUT THIS STORY IS...

I THINK THIS BOOK IS...

WHICH IS WHY I GIVE IT THIS MANY STARS

WOULD I READ IT AGAIN?

Start Date: _______________   End Date: _______________

THE BOOK I READ IS...

THE AUTHOR IS...

THE STORY IS ABOUT...

MY FAVORITE CHARACTER IS ...

BECAUSE ...

WHAT I LIKED ABOUT THIS
STORY IS...

WHAT I DISLIKED ABOUT THIS
STORY IS...

I THINK THIS BOOK IS...

WHICH IS WHY I GIVE IT THIS MANY STARS

WOULD I READ IT AGAIN?

Start Date: _______________   End Date: _______________

THE BOOK I READ IS...

THE AUTHOR IS...

THE STORY IS ABOUT...

MY FAVORITE CHARACTER IS ...

BECAUSE ...

WHAT I LIKED ABOUT THIS
STORY IS...

WHAT I DISLIKED ABOUT THIS
STORY IS...

I THINK THIS BOOK IS...

WHICH IS WHY I GIVE IT THIS MANY STARS

WOULD I READ IT AGAIN?

Start Date: _______________   End Date: _______________

THE BOOK I READ IS...

THE AUTHOR IS...

THE STORY IS ABOUT...

MY FAVORITE CHARACTER IS ...

BECAUSE ...

WHAT I LIKED ABOUT THIS
STORY IS...

WHAT I DISLIKED ABOUT THIS
STORY IS...

I THINK THIS BOOK IS...

WHICH IS WHY I GIVE IT THIS MANY STARS

WOULD I READ IT AGAIN?

Start Date: _______________   **End Date:** _______________

THE BOOK I READ IS...

THE AUTHOR IS...

THE STORY IS ABOUT...

MY FAVORITE CHARACTER IS ...

BECAUSE ...

WHAT I LIKED ABOUT THIS
STORY IS...

WHAT I DISLIKED ABOUT THIS
STORY IS...

I THINK THIS BOOK IS...

WHICH IS WHY I GIVE IT THIS MANY STARS

WOULD I READ IT AGAIN?

Start Date: _______________   End Date: _______________

THE BOOK I READ IS...

THE AUTHOR IS...

THE STORY IS ABOUT...

MY FAVORITE CHARACTER IS ...

BECAUSE ...

WHAT I LIKED ABOUT THIS STORY IS...

WHAT I DISLIKED ABOUT THIS STORY IS...

I THINK THIS BOOK IS...

WHICH IS WHY I GIVE IT THIS MANY STARS

WOULD I READ IT AGAIN?

Start Date: ________________   **End Date:** ________________

THE BOOK I READ IS...

THE AUTHOR IS...

THE STORY IS ABOUT...

MY FAVORITE CHARACTER IS ...

BECAUSE ...

WHAT I LIKED ABOUT THIS
STORY IS...

WHAT I DISLIKED ABOUT THIS
STORY IS...

I THINK THIS BOOK IS...

WHICH IS WHY I GIVE IT THIS MANY STARS

WOULD I READ IT AGAIN?

Start Date: _______________   End Date: _______________

THE BOOK I READ IS...

THE AUTHOR IS...

THE STORY IS ABOUT...

MY FAVORITE CHARACTER IS ...

BECAUSE ...

WHAT I LIKED ABOUT THIS
STORY IS...

WHAT I DISLIKED ABOUT THIS
STORY IS...

I THINK THIS BOOK IS...

WHICH IS WHY I GIVE IT THIS MANY STARS

WOULD I READ IT AGAIN?

Start Date: _______________   End Date: _______________

THE BOOK I READ IS...

THE AUTHOR IS...

THE STORY IS ABOUT...

MY FAVORITE CHARACTER IS ...

BECAUSE ...

WHAT I LIKED ABOUT THIS
STORY IS...

WHAT I DISLIKED ABOUT THIS
STORY IS...

I THINK THIS BOOK IS...

WHICH IS WHY I GIVE IT THIS MANY STARS

WOULD I READ IT AGAIN?

Start Date: ______________   End Date: ______________

THE BOOK I READ IS...

THE AUTHOR IS...

THE STORY IS ABOUT...

MY FAVORITE CHARACTER IS ...

BECAUSE ...

WHAT I LIKED ABOUT THIS STORY IS...

WHAT I DISLIKED ABOUT THIS STORY IS...

I THINK THIS BOOK IS...

WHICH IS WHY I GIVE IT THIS MANY STARS

WOULD I READ IT AGAIN?

Start Date: _______________   **End Date:** _______________

THE BOOK I READ IS...

THE AUTHOR IS...

THE STORY IS ABOUT...

MY FAVORITE CHARACTER IS ...

BECAUSE ...

WHAT I LIKED ABOUT THIS
STORY IS...

WHAT I DISLIKED ABOUT THIS
STORY IS...

I THINK THIS BOOK IS...

WHICH IS WHY I GIVE IT THIS MANY STARS

WOULD I READ IT AGAIN?

Start Date: _______________   End Date: _______________

THE BOOK I READ IS...

THE AUTHOR IS...

THE STORY IS ABOUT...

MY FAVORITE CHARACTER IS ...

BECAUSE ...

WHAT I LIKED ABOUT THIS STORY IS...

WHAT I DISLIKED ABOUT THIS STORY IS...

I THINK THIS BOOK IS...

WHICH IS WHY I GIVE IT THIS MANY STARS

WOULD I READ IT AGAIN?

Start Date: _______________   End Date: _______________

THE BOOK I READ IS...

THE AUTHOR IS...

THE STORY IS ABOUT...

MY FAVORITE CHARACTER IS ...

 BECAUSE ...

WHAT I LIKED ABOUT THIS
STORY IS...

WHAT I DISLIKED ABOUT THIS
STORY IS...

I THINK THIS BOOK IS...

WHICH IS WHY I GIVE IT THIS MANY STARS

WOULD I READ IT AGAIN?

Start Date: ________________   End Date: ________________

THE BOOK I READ IS...

THE AUTHOR IS...

THE STORY IS ABOUT...

MY FAVORITE CHARACTER IS ...

BECAUSE ...

WHAT I LIKED ABOUT THIS STORY IS...   WHAT I DISLIKED ABOUT THIS STORY IS...

I THINK THIS BOOK IS...

WHICH IS WHY I GIVE IT THIS MANY STARS

WOULD I READ IT AGAIN?

Start Date: _______________   End Date: _______________

THE BOOK I READ IS...

THE AUTHOR IS...

THE STORY IS ABOUT...

MY FAVORITE CHARACTER IS ...

BECAUSE ...

WHAT I LIKED ABOUT THIS
STORY IS...

WHAT I DISLIKED ABOUT THIS
STORY IS...

I THINK THIS BOOK IS...

WHICH IS WHY I GIVE IT THIS MANY STARS

WOULD I READ IT AGAIN?

Start Date: _________________   End Date: _________________

THE BOOK I READ IS...

THE AUTHOR IS...

THE STORY IS ABOUT...

MY FAVORITE CHARACTER IS ...

BECAUSE ...

WHAT I LIKED ABOUT THIS STORY IS...

WHAT I DISLIKED ABOUT THIS STORY IS...

I THINK THIS BOOK IS...

WHICH IS WHY I GIVE IT THIS MANY STARS

WOULD I READ IT AGAIN?

Start Date: ________________   End Date: ________________

THE BOOK I READ IS...

THE AUTHOR IS...

THE STORY IS ABOUT...

MY FAVORITE CHARACTER IS ...

BECAUSE ...

WHAT I LIKED ABOUT THIS STORY IS...

WHAT I DISLIKED ABOUT THIS STORY IS...

I THINK THIS BOOK IS...

WHICH IS WHY I GIVE IT THIS MANY STARS

WOULD I READ IT AGAIN?

Thank you

We hope you enjoyed our book

For us, your feedback is very important
Please let us know how you liked our book at:

oliviabrooks2222@gmail.com

Hope to see you again